Synonyms and Antonyms

Revised

© C.R. Draper 2018

First published, achieve2day, Slough, 2015

Revised version published: achieve2day, Slough, 2018

ISBN: 978-1-909986-13-8

Synonyms and Antonyms

A synonym is a word with the same or nearly the same meaning. Antonyms are words that have the opposite or nearly the opposite meaning.

Synonyms and antonyms are extremely common in 11 Plus exams.

Synonyms and antonyms appear in the 11 Plus in the following ways:
- Choosing the most similar (or most opposite) words from two sets of words.
- Choosing the synonym (or antonym) of a word from a small number of options.
- Completing the synonym (or antonym) by filling in the missing letters.
- In cloze exercises.

This book has a number of pages that ask you to put words into groups of synonyms. This is because most words have more than one synonym and rather than learning each one separately, it is easier to learn the words as a group. Most of these pages contain two sets of synonyms, each set containing the antonyms to the other set. This allows you to make a lot of connections in just one page.

Since spelling and vocabulary is vital to success in the 11 Plus, to increase your vocabulary it is important to look up any words you do not know. Due to the large amount of work when preparing for the 11 Plus and the large number of words that you need to become familiar with, I recommend an electronic method to look up words, if possible.

Further, it is a good idea, as you work through this book to make a note of any words that you do not know and their definition. This will help you build a useful list of words that will be helpful for you to know for the 11 Plus examination.

All the best in your studies.

Christine Draper.

1. Laugh or Cry

Put the following words in the correct column below:

Word bank:

giggle, chortle, weep, chuckle, sob, wail, guffaw, bawl, snicker, howl, snivel, crack up, cackle, mewl

laugh	cry
Chuckle	Weep
giggle	Sob
chortle	bawl
guffaw	wail
snicker	howl
Crack up	snivel
cackle	mewl

2. Synonyms

Choose the synonym of the word in bold.

1. **belated**   punctual, time, <u>tardy,</u> slow

2. **wide**   <u>broad</u>, narrow, thin, perish

3. **summit**   hill, mountain, <u>peak,</u> base, nadir

4. **consent**   choose, <u>agree</u>, confine, include

5. **open**   closed, sealed, <u>ajar</u>, wide, accord

6. **patient**   doctor, indifferent, <u>tolerant</u>, genteel

7. **blend**   sew, gather, colour, method, <u>mix</u>

8. **scruffy**   meagre, <u>shabby</u>, dingy, tired, fresh

9. **legend**   <u>table</u>, image, caption, axis, superior

10. **rude**   polite, talk, adverse, <u>insolent</u>, solvent

3. Antonyms

Complete the antonym of the word in bold.

1. **wrong**   c o r r e c t

2. **notice**   i g n o r e

3. **best**   w o r s t

4. **begin**   c o n c l u d e

5. **allow**   d e n y

6. **separate**   m e r g e

7. **horizontal**   v e r t i c a l

8. **clean**   f i l t h y

9. **break**   r e p a i r

10. **consent**   o b j e c t

4. Happy and Sad

Put the following words in the correct column below:

Word bank: upset, miserable, content, pitiful, joyful, cheerful, glad, lament, distress, pleased, depressed, upbeat, elated, melancholy, jubilant, delighted, dismayed, desolate, gleeful, glum

happy	sad
_____	_____
_____	_____
_____	_____
_____	_____
_____	_____
_____	_____
_____	_____
_____	_____
_____	_____

Which word also means the following?
Information made available,
Things held or included in something.   _____

A sad poem
A complaint   _____

5. Synonyms

Complete the synonym of the word in bold.

1. **untidy**   m e _ _ _

2. **prize**   a _ _ _ d

3. **break**   i n t _ _ _ _ l

4. **flat**   l _ _ _ l

5. **smart**   i n t _ _ _ _ _ _ _ t

6. **eager**   e n t _ _ _ _ _ _ t i c

7. **gulp**   s w _ _ _ o w

8. **think**   c _ _ _ _ _ e r

9. **shade**   t _ _ _

10. **want**   d _ _ _ _ e

6. Antonyms

Choose the antonym of the word in bold.

1. **firm**   business, soft, solid, sponge

2. **boil**   anger, temper, freeze, emotion

3. **guilty**   innocent, innocuous, metal, create

4. **parallel**   side, horizontal, perpendicular, tall

5. **initial**   final, first, consultation, value

6. **penalty**   punish, work, discover, reward

7. **straight**   thin, path, bumpy, wavy

8. **violent**   fierce, wild, shy, gentle

9. **shiny**   mat, dull, glow, radiant

10. **taut**   learned, find, slack, slow

7. Lots and Few

Put the following words in the correct column below:

Word bank:

lean, numerous, slight, trifle, scanty, plentiful, meagre, plenty, myriad, many, negligible, populous, paltry, several, sparse, oodles, copious, scarce

lots	few

8. Synonyms

Choose the synonym of the word in bold.

1. **give**   take, reply, donate, charity

2. **circle**   shape, surround, fence, square

3. **amend**   improve, deficient, consider, deceive

4. **woman**   female, lady, man, girl

5. **confident**   happy, correct, assured, threaten

6. **trench**   coat, spade, veto, channel

7. **bend**   flexible, warp, break, rules

8. **dirty**   clean, mud, muddy, soiled

9. **lose**   loose, misplace, lost, found

10. **debate**   talk, think, discuss, conclude

9. Antonyms

Complete the antonym of the word in bold.

1. **obvious**   s u _ _ _ e

2. **clear**   o _ _ _ u e

3. **enlarge**   _ _ _ _ _ n k

4. **loss**   p _ _ _ _ t

5. **sink**   _ l _ _ t

6. **common**   u n _ _ _ e

7. **alert**   d r _ _ _ _

8. **vain**   _ _ _ e s t

9. **sour**   s w _ _ _

10. **begin**   c _ _ _ e

10.   Wise Folly

Put the following words in the correct column below:

Word bank: clever, bright, dumb, doltish, intelligent, dopey, wise, shrewd, silly, astute, witless, imbecile, brilliant, unintelligent, genius, inane, savvy, unwise, ludicrous, sage

smart	stupid

11. Synonyms

Complete the synonym of the word in bold.

1. **twelve**   _ _ _ e n

2. **elevate**   r _ _ _ e

3. **fear**   _ r e _ _

4. **myth**   _ _ b l _

5. **find**   _ _ s c o _ _ _

6. **calm**   t r _ _ _ _ i l

7. **assessment**   e v _ _ _ _ t i o n

8. **trick**   d e _ _ _ _ e

9. **choice**   _ p t _ _ n

10. **sure**   c _ _ _ _ i n

12. Antonyms

Choose the antonym of the word in bold.

1. **real** illusion, deceit, novel, genuine

2. **support** structure, periphery, betray, help

3. **confident** nerves, nervous, scared, eager

4. **wary** gullible, berate, baffle, contract

5. **simple** easy, fine, fancy, complex

6. **strong** thin, light, brittle, flexible

7. **stride** walk, pace, idle, shuffle

8. **complete** partial, like, inclusive, miserly

9. **show** find, play, hidden, conceal

10. **plenty** narrow, wide, slight, sparse

13.   Movement

Put the following words in the correct column below:

Word bank:

mobile, motion, stationary, active, inaction, immobile,
ambulatory, stable, stagnant, locomotive

move	still
_____	_____
_____	_____
_____	_____
_____	_____
_____	_____

Which word also means the following?

A child's toy hung from the ceiling   _____

A still lake or pond   _____

A place where horses are kept.   _____

One of the words is the homophone for pens and paper. What is
the word used for pens and paper? _____

14.   Synonyms

Choose the synonym of the word in bold.

1. **barb**   hook, metal, wire, acquire

2. **despair**   single, happy, anguish, fear

3. **next**   ascend, after, subsequent, suffice

4. **unkind**   cruel, caring, hate, contempt

5. **possible**   success, obstacle, augment, achievable

6. **understand**   knew, mature, comprehend, competent

7. **string**   twist, twine, wind, fastener

8. **disclose**   revel, find, reveal, replete

9. **peripheral**   merge, limit, marginal, flexible

10. **combine**   include, blend, gather, comply

15.   Antonyms

Complete the antonym of the word in bold.

1. **juvenile**   m _ _ _ r e

2. **threw**   _ _ _ _ h t

3. **believe**   d o _ _ _

4. **lead**   _ _ l l o _

5. **reject**   _ _ c e p _

6. **order**   c h _ _ _

7. **innocent**   _ _ _ l t y

8. **bitter**   s w _ _ _

9. **full**   e m _ _ _

10. **unravel**   t a _ g _ _

16.   Hungry and Sated

Put the following words in the correct column below:

Word bank: ravenous, full, peckish, starving, replete, famished, satisfied, satiated

hungry	sated
_____	_____
_____	_____
_____	_____
_____	_____

Note: Hungry and thirsty can be both synonyms and antonyms. They can both mean wanting something e.g. thirst for knowledge or hungry for recognition.

Which word above means only a little bit hungry? _____

Which word is a synonym of contented or pleased? _____

Which words are synonyms of full?   _____

                                                     _____

19

17.   Synonyms

Complete the synonym of the word in bold.

1. **sleepy**   d _ _ w _ _

2. **leave**   a b _ _ _ _ n

3. **conflict**   b _ _ _ l e

4. **brief**   c o _ _ _ _ e

5. **coax**   p e r _ _ _ _ e

6. **colossus**   _ _ _ n t

7. **thrifty**   f r _ _ _ _

8. **pharmacy**   _ _ e m i s _

9. **success**   v i _ _ _ _ y

10. **tire**   e x _ _ _ _ t

18. Antonyms

Choose the antonym of the word in bold.

1. **lower**   addition, elevate, order, high

2. **contradict**   malady, cease, crave, agree

3. **static**   electric, dynamic, engine, country

4. **live**   deed, house, dead, still

5. **competent**   inept, intrigue, enthral, insulate

6. **exceptional**   amazing, insulting, mediocre, sanction

7. **coherent**   rational, irrational, logical, jeer

8. **optional**   instigate, compulsory, inspiring, eager

9. **awkward**   elevate, cooperate, ungainly, dextrous

10. **strict**   calm, lenient, patient, antagonise

19. Approximately spot-on

Put the following words in the correct column below:

Word bank: obscure, undefined, precise, accurate, perfect, faint, specific, shadowy, ambiguous, dubious, detailed, definite, meticulous, equivocal, rigorous, sharp, uncertain, unclear, scrupulous, nebulous

exact	vague

20. Synonyms

Choose the synonym of the word in bold.

1. **limit**   preserve, restrain, negate, extend

2. **berate**   chastise, memorial, paramount, laugh

3. **empty**   crave, contradict, abandon, deplete

4. **defy**   resist, mock, regard, negligent

5. **glut**   wheat, intolerance, fill, surplus

6. **permeate**   pierce, ramble, penetrate, shrews

7. **settle**   neglect, hesitate, establish, haughty

8. **imitate**   glare, copy, affirm, vouch

9. **pliable**   tools, grasp, durable, flexible

10. **baffle**   confuse, fence, insolent, nimble

21.   Antonyms

Complete the antonym of the word in bold.

1. **capture**   r _ _ _ _ s e

2. **advance**   _ _ _ r e a t

3. **compliment**   i n _ _ _ _ _

4. **professional**   a m _ _ _ _ r

5. **cellar**   a _ _ _ _

6. **tragedy**   _ _ _ e d y

7. **transparent**   o p _ _ _ _ _

8. **triumph**   _ _ _ e a t

9. **public**   p _ _ _ _ t e

10. **arrive**   d _ _ _ _ t

22.   When?

Put the following words in the correct column below:

> Word bank: subsequently, former, later, prior, earlier, afterwards, ensuing, ahead, previously, succeeding, thereafter, preliminary

before	after
_____	_____
_____	_____
_____	_____
_____	_____
_____	_____
_____	_____

Which word above would fit best in the sentence below?

He prepared thoroughly _____ of time.

23.   Synonyms

Complete the synonym of the word in bold.

1. extract   r e _ _ _ _

2. cinch   e _ _ _

3. accident   _ r a _ _

4. hut   _ _ _ c k

5. own   p o _ _ _ _ s

6. baby   _ _ _ _ n t

7. gift   p r _ _ _ _ t

8. late   t _ _ _ y

9. abrupt   _ _ _ d e n

10. just   f _ _ _

24.   Antonyms

Choose the antonym of the word in bold.

1. **abolish**   sustain, terminate, demolish, endure

2. **even**   flat, smooth, difficult, odd

3. **annoy**   anger, soothe, sane, forgive

4. **refute**   confirm, litter, useful, propose

5. **patient**   approach, forbearing, agitated, stingy

6. **novice**   new, old, expert, fortune

7. **stabilise**   descend, upset, insult, optimal

8. **urge**   encourage, sturdy, exclude, deter

9. **minor**   child, older, major, chord

10. **folly**   wisdom, build, choose, crease

25.   Let's Clean Up

Put the following words in the correct column below:

Word bank: clear, filth, unclouded, soil, contaminate, dingy, uncontaminated, neat, pristine, grime, stain, washed

clean	dirt
_____	_____
_____	_____
_____	_____
_____	_____
_____	_____
_____	_____

Which word also means the following?

Part of the Earth's surface   _____

Exceptionally clean   _____

26.   Synonyms

Choose the synonym of the word in bold.

1. **raucous**   thick, loud, cheap, discard

2. **indolent**   lazy, small, rude, painful

3. **dismal**   humiliate, justify, miser, dingy

4. **shun**   berth, sanction, avoid, confront

5. **forgo**   depart, abstain, indulge, reject

6. **club**   spade, stick, trench, baton

7. **deteriorate**   decline, break, conflict, chaotic

8. **turbulent**   calm, technical, engine, stormy

9. **isolated**   public, forlorn, deserted, included

10. **inquire**   agree, ask, implore, away

27.   Antonyms

Complete the antonym of the word in bold.

1. **loose**   t i _ _ _

2. **bold**   t i _ _ _

3. **artificial** n a _ _ _ _ l

4. **smile**   _ _ _ w n

5. **rural**   u _ _ _ _

6. **attack**   _ _ _ e n d

7. **floor**   _ _ _ l i n g

8. **import**   _ _ _ o r t

9. **clear**   c l _ _ _ _

10. **lend**   b o r _ _ _

28.   Break a Leg

Put the following words in the correct column below:

| Word bank: fortunate, unfortunate, unfavourable, favourable, felicitous, prosperous, doomed, ill-fated, luckless, fortuitous, blessed, hapless |

lucky	unlucky

What does the saying "break a leg" at the top of this page mean?

_____

29. Synonyms

Complete the synonym of the word in bold.

1. **centre**   _ _ _ d l e

2. **faithful**   l _ _ _ _ _

3. **weak**   _ _ _ _ l e

4. **capacity**   _ _ l u m _

5. **overseas**   a _ _ _ _ d

6. **change**   _ _ _ _ s f o r m

7. **collect**   g a _ _ _ _ _

8. **dash**   s p _ _ _ _ _

9. **glitter**   _ _ _ _ k l e

10. **imitate**   m i _ _ _

30.   Antonyms

Choose the antonym of the word in bold.

1. **fair**   alike, gloomy, biased, accused

2. **indulge**   deprive, coddle, satiate, oblige

3. **dusk**   start, dawn, late, sparkling

4. **dry**   tepid, humid, wring, alcohol

5. **harvest**   bush, tree, plant, crop

6. **success**   fail, subtract, shame, failure

7. **supporter**   opponent, disagree, against, attack

8. **rise**   low, fast, slow, sink

9. **criticism**   praise, random, segregate, superb

10. **quality**   rigid, flexible, unstable, inferior

31.   No Sitting on the Fence

Put the following words in the correct column below:

Word bank: concur, differ, accord, dissent, discord, tally, concord, refuse, contradict, match, diverge, consent, clash, accept, assent, counter

agree	disagree

What does the saying "to sit on the fence" mean?

_____

32. Synonyms

Choose the synonym of the word in bold.

1. **contrary** disagreeable, difference, planned, seize

2. **keen** mustard, dressing, eager, fast

3. **function** calculate, operate, marquee, entertain

4. **quota** allocate, factory, allowance, bloat

5. **book** order, atlas, read, provide

6. **dispute** derelict, decision, motivate, argue

7. **distant** develop, far, temporary, though

8. **status** position, location, statue, occupy

9. **ingredient** part, component, contemplate, recipe

10. **immaculate** strict, created, desire, perfect

33.   Antonyms

Complete the antonym of the word in bold.

1. midnight   n _ _ _

2. save   s p _ _ _

3. senior   _ _ _ i o r

4. vowel   _ _ _ _ o n a n t

5. serious   _ _ _ n y

6. sharp   b _ _ _ t

7. often   s e l _ _ _

8. man   w o _ _ _

9. cheerful   s o _ _ _ _ _

10. cold   t _ _ _ _ y

34.   By and By, in the Fullness of Time

Put the following words in the correct column below:

Word bank: immediately, today, whenever, someday,
intermittently, instantly, occasional, periodically, straightaway,
directly, forthwith, sporadically

now	sometime
_____	_____
_____	_____
_____	_____
_____	_____
_____	_____
_____	_____

Which word can mean "at regular intervals of time"?

_____

35.   Synonyms

Complete the synonym of the word in bold.

1. **hate**   d e _ _ _ _ _

2. **kin**   r e _ _ _ _ _ e

3. **foretell**   _ _ _ _ i c t

4. **heed**   c o n _ _ _ _ r

5. **isolation**   s o l _ _ _ _ e

6. **banish**   e x _ _ _

7. **throng**   c r _ _ _

8. **skill**   t a _ _ _ _

9. **aloof**   d i s _ _ _ _

10. **congregate**   g a _ _ _ _

36.   Antonyms

Choose the antonym of the word in bold.

1. **cautious**   illogical, reckless, thoughtless, enrage

2. **perilous**   safe, similar, decay, clever

3. **overt**   open, closed, secret, shallow

4. **candid**   unkind, blunt, pretend, dishonest

5. **stingy**   wasteful, sparse, liberal, attract

6. **omit**   neglect, include find, decoy

7. **functional**   futile, useful, thwart, impede

8. **contempt**   like, awe, overt, pique

9. **luminous**   light, reflect, dim, despair

10. **kindle**   smother, light, placid, excite

37.   I'm Rather Partial to Fractions

Put the following words in the correct column below:

Word bank: complete, entire, part, total, piece, section, sector, altogether, division, unit, full, fragment

fraction	whole

Which word is a homophone for peace? _____

38.   Synonyms

Choose the synonym of the word in bold.

1. **gracious**   pleasant, clever, pretty, upright

2. **pensive**   caged, oppressed, thoughtful, sad

3. **remote**   automatic, distant, toy, mobile

4. **impel**   force, hinder, startle, manifest

5. **malign**   straighten, mess, crooked, slander

6. **impartial**   biased, like, fair, worried

7. **best**   good, success, assured, elite

8. **assault**   contempt, attack, injured, victim

9. **hover**   float, wait, waft, blink

10. **vapour**   exhale, mist, humid, damp

39.   Antonyms

Complete the antonym of the word in bold.

1. **worse**   _ _ _ t e r

2. **host**   g _ _ _ _

3. **advance**   _ _ _ _ d r a w

4. **obtuse**   a _ _ _ _

5. **sullen**   _ _ _ _ r f u l

6. **abridge**   e x _ _ _ _

7. **continue**   p _ _ _ e

8. **rest**   l a _ _ _ _

9. **lengthy**   c _ _ _ i s e

10. **keep**   d i s _ _ _ _

40.   Ready for Bed

Put the following words in the correct column below:

Word bank: weary, fatigue, lively, jaded, fresh, activated, invigorated, exhausted, drained, refreshed, rested, drowsy

tired	energised
_____	_____
_____	_____
_____	_____
_____	_____
_____	_____
_____	_____

Which word?

Means extremely tired   _____

Opposite of stale   _____

41.   Synonyms

Complete the synonym of the word in bold.

1. **give**   d _ _ _ t e

2. **select**   c h _ _ _ _

3. **slack**   l _ _ _ e

4. **mistake**   e _ _ _ r

5. **pile**   h _ _ _

6. **odd**   u _ _ _ _ a l

7. **limp**   _ l o _ _ y

8. **power**   m _ _ _ t

9. **essential**   v i _ _ _

10. **rapid**   s _ _ _ t

42.   Antonyms

Choose the antonym of the word in bold.

1. **meagre**   scant, kind, generous, copious

2. **famous**   poor, miser, obscure, untalented

3. **spurn**   crave, affirm, defeat, victory

4. **granted**   found, lost, repute, refused

5. **sea**   pond, land, river, fresh

6. **neglect**   care, success, disdain, careless

7. **prohibit**   fresh, permit, ticket, probate

8. **robust**   light, meagre, slight, flimsy

9. **dawdle**   draw, paint, rush, paltry

10. **verify**   refute, scoff, approve, flout

43.   At the Marketplace

Put the following words in the correct column below:

Word bank: purchase, market, acquire, auction, get, peddle, hawk, invest, stock, obtain, procure, vend

buy	sell

Which word above is also a bird of prey? _____

44.   Synonyms

Choose the synonym of the word in bold.

1. **distort**   change, harm, deform, waste

2. **pivotal**   important, turn, straight, steady

3. **perceive**   confine, indefinite, recognise, contrived

4. **patient**   doctor, caring, polite, tireless

5. **modest**   honourable, humble, pious, familiar

6. **hurdle**   barrier, race, squat, assist

7. **sincere**   superficial, dissuade, earnest, true

8. **temperate**   hot, humid, pleasant, extreme

9. **irksome**   delight, annoying, cruel, impartial

10. **evidence**   stand, report, expose, proof

45.   Antonyms

Complete the antonym of the word in bold.

1. descendant   a n _ _ _ _ o r

2. knowledgeable   i _ _ _ _ a n c e

3. distant   a d _ _ _ _ _ n t

4. graceful   a w _ _ _ r d

5. continue   _ _ _ e r r u p _

6. sparse   d _ _ _ e

7. remember   _ _ _ g e t

8. aware   _ _ _ i v i o u s

9. support   _ _ _ o s e

10. affluence   p o _ _ _ t y

46.   Bigger and Smaller

Put the following words in the correct column below:

Word bank: grow, inflate, shrink, amplify, deflate, compress, enlarge, dilate, constrict, magnify, compact, reduce

expand	contract
_____	_____
_____	_____
_____	_____
_____	_____
_____	_____
_____	_____

Which word can be used to mean:

Make sound louder? _____

Put air into a tyre? _____

47. Synonyms

Complete the synonym of the word in bold.

1. **wash**   c l _ _ _ _ e

2. **odd**   b i _ _ _ _ e

3. **hinder**   _ _ _ t r u c t

4. **disclose**   _ _ _ e a l

5. **handbook**   m a _ _ _ l

6. **lea**   _ _ _ d o w

7. **peak**   p i n _ _ _ _ e

8. **change**   m o _ _ _ y

9. **persist**   e n _ _ _ e

10. **exchange** r e _ _ _ _ e

48.   Antonyms

Choose the antonym of the word in bold.

1. **perimeter**   circumference, interior, border, circuit

2. **ostentatious**   obvious, adorned, grimy, discreet

3. **defy**   deceit, receipt, traitor, obey

4. **liberate**   flourish, oppress, volatile, detrimental

5. **domestic**   internal, foreign, home, deserter

6. **aggravation**   solace, dignify, gripping, brazen

7. **flee**   insect, bird, escape, capture

8. **extinguish**   water, enlarge, inflame, blaze

9. **sharp**   quick, slow, thick, blunt

10. **thwart**   carry, neglect, enable, working

49.   Good, Better, Best

Put the following words in the correct column below:

Word bank: nice, nasty, vile, pleasant, horrible, despicable, foul, delightful, gratifying, marvellous, sterling, obnoxious, proficient, repulsive, loathsome, adept, odious, beneficial, atrocious, agreeable

good	bad

50.   Synonyms

Choose the synonym of the word in bold.

1. **foundation**   basis, centre, explain, research

2. **wavering**   farewell, regard, hesitant, friendly

3. **fissure**   extinct, muddle, clear, crack

4. **engaging**   boring, riveting, poised, occupied

5. **disguise**   devout, horrible, camouflage, derelict

6. **imposing**   danger, protected, boisterous, dramatic

7. **augment**   add, allow, let, admit

8. **youth**   mature, berate, infant, adolescent

9. **crave**   ache, yearn, hunger, goal

10. **conspicuous**   correct, obvious, hidden, costly

51.   Antonyms

Complete the antonym of the word in bold.

1. occupied   v a _ _ _ t

2. often   s e l _ _ _

3. supply   d e m _ _ _

4. credit   _ _ _ i t

5. suppress   p r o m _ _ _

6. prose   p o _ _ _ y

7. relaxed   t e _ _ _

8. solid   h o _ _ o _

9. deep   s h _ _ _ _ _

10. exit   _ _ _ _ _ n c e

52.   Bone Idle

Put the following words in the correct column below:

> Word bank: inactive, slack, industrious, conscientious, idle, diligent, productive, indolent, lackadaisical, unproductive, busy, lax, tireless, assiduous

active	lazy

53.   Synonyms

Complete the synonym of the word in bold.

1. **apparent**   v i _ _ _ _ e

2. **fade**   d w i _ _ _ _

3. **pious**   d e _ _ _ t

4. **blame**   a c _ _ _ e

5. **tolerate**   e n _ _ _ e

6. **altitude**   h _ _ _ h t

7. **irate**   f u _ _ _ _ _

8. **confirm**   v e _ _ _ _

9. **assemble**   c o n _ _ _ _ _ t

10. **definite**   c e r _ _ _ _

54.   Antonyms

Choose the antonym of the word in bold.

1. **unkempt**   forgotten, thrown, rubbish, tidy

2. **lawful**   legitimate, illegal, legislate, disallow

3. **subordinate** stormy, excellent, superior, dirty

4. **chaotic**   ordered, desist, division, grant

5. **placate**   pacify, reconcile, irritate, mollify

6. **tame**   angry, wild, difficult, eager

7. **achievable** diminish, intentional, impossible, refuse

8. **abnormal**   conventional, impartial, validate, correct

9. **wax**   increasing, bee, vanity, wane

10. **profligate** careful, acquire, take, frugal

55.   In Need of Repair

Put the following words in the correct column below:

Word bank: break, fix, mend, fracture, rupture, patch, harm, impair, reconstruct, wreck, improve, restore

damage	repair
_____	_____
_____	_____
_____	_____
_____	_____
_____	_____
_____	_____

Which word can also mean:
- interval
- fissure / opening   _____

Which word can also mean a dilemma?   _____

56.   Synonyms

Choose the synonym of the word in bold.

1. **curb**   road, path, limit, speed

2. **convey**   forth, transport, choose, protect

3. **eccentric**   sole, competent, authentic, unusual

4. **allowance**   cheap, budget, inexpensive, economy

5. **stabilise**   balance, sanction, upbeat, apathy

6. **lucid**   clearly, category, derive, concur

7. **coarse**   agree, compulsory, rough, study

8. **bright**   fist, dazzling, talent, stupid

9. **brilliant**   creative, classify, splendid, good

10. **flatter**   complement, tickle, sweet, compliment

57.   Antonyms

Complete the antonym of the word in bold.

1. **accidental**   i n _ _ _ _ i o n a l

2. **lofty**   l _ _ _ y

3. **shopkeeper**   c u _ _ _ _ e r

4. **compulsory**   _ _ _ _ n t a r y

5. **childish**   m _ _ _ r e

6. **ascend**   _ _ _ c e n d

7. **start**   _ _ _ _ l u d e

8. **left**   r i _ _ _

9. **landlord**   t e _ _ _ t

10. **diminish**   i n _ _ _ _ s e

58.   Open and Shut

Put the following words in the correct column below:

Word bank: aperture, cavity, cleft, sealed, shut, crack, crevice, impenetrable, cut, impermeable, blocked, firm, fissure, hatch, tight, secure, rift, impervious, rupture, fixed, fast, slit, fastened, slot, corked, locked, tear, vent

opening	closed

59. Synonyms

Complete the synonym of the word in bold.

1. **comprise**   i n c _ _ _ _

2. **agree**   c o n _ _ _

3. **treatment**   r e _ _ _ _

4. **auspicious**   h o _ _ _ u l

5. **wander**   r a _ _ _ e

6. **majestic**   r e _ _ _

7. **trivial**   p e _ _ _

8. **immerse**   s u b _ _ _ _ e

9. **decipher**   d e _ _ _ e

10. **loft**   a t _ _ _

60.   Antonyms

Choose the antonym of the word in bold.

1. **negate**   agree, validate, contradict, know

2. **veto**   sanction, together, antagonise, calm

3. **apathy**   pleasant, calm, agitated, interest

4. **paramount**   mounted, over, coward, minimal

5. **riveting**   spanner, screws, tedious, talented

6. **perpetuate**   confuse, unsure, discontinue, conserve

7. **incapable**   learn, success, agree, able

8. **betrayal**   loyalty, eligible, sincere, cherish

9. **evil**   justify, alarm, right, good

10. **cherish**   adore, despise, despair, cruel

61.   There's No Doubt

Put the following words in the correct column below:

Word bank: fear, hesitation, assurance, uncertainty, certainty, boldness, cowardice, fortitude, fearlessness, timidity, apprehension, grit

confidence	doubt
_____	_____
_____	_____
_____	_____
_____	_____
_____	_____
_____	_____

Which word can also mean small loose particles
of stone or sand?   _____

62.   Synonyms

Choose the synonym of the word in bold.

1. **accept**   receive, choose, decline, approach

2. **private**   imprison, public, confidential, unknown

3. **labyrinth**   paths, maze, magical, wolf

4. **imperative** unnecessary, essential, accidental, lout

5. **ancillary**   additional, salary, cellars, staff

6. **viscous**   harsh, halt, liquid, thick

7. **swollen**   turbulent, gravely, bloated, infected

8. **shelter**   hide, campsite, harbour, captive

9. **ancestral**   ancient, inherited, bestow, ancestor

10. **evident**   unclear, ambiguous, brazen, obvious

63.   Antonyms

Complete the antonym of the word in bold.

1. **right**   w _ _ _ g

2. **persuade**   _ _ _ _ u a d e

3. **introduction** _ _ _ _ l u s i o n

4. **sorry**   p l _ _ _ _ d

5. **tardy**   p u _ _ _ u a l

6. **treasure**   n e _ _ _ _ t

7. **absent**   _ _ _ _ e n t

8. **constant**   v a _ _ _ _ l e

9. **deteriorate**   t h _ _ _ e

10. **weak**   s t u _ _ _

64.   To Love

Put the following words in the correct column below:

Word bank: adore, despise, animosity, cherish, fondness, besotted, dislike, enmity, relish, abhor, admire, loathe

love	hate
_____	_____
_____	_____
_____	_____
_____	_____
_____	_____
_____	_____

Which word can also mean a condiment?   _____

65.   Synonyms

Complete the synonym of the word in bold.

1. **inevitable**   c e r _ _ _ _ _

2. **firm**   c o m _ _ _ y

3. **enormous**   g i _ _ _ _ _ i c

4. **student**   p u _ _ _

5. **teach**   i n s _ _ _ _ _ t

6. **satisfactory**   a l r _ _ _ _ _

7. **site**   s c _ _ _

8. **label**   t i _ _ _ t

9. **silly**   f o _ _ _ _ _ h

10. **jumped**   l e _ _ _

66.   Antonyms

Choose the antonym of the word in bold.

1. **demean**   humiliate, uplift, grew, positive

2. **averse**   reluctant, hostile, contrary, agreeable

3. **never**   always, occasionally, often, soon

4. **fresh**   mouldy, rotten, stale, dank

5. **discount**   reduce, decrease, ignore, accept

6. **rigid**   adapted, stiff, supple, bend

7. **noble**   imperial, gentle, genteel, lowly

8. **smooth**   shiny, wrinkled, gloss, matte

9. **apparent**   vague, disappear, obvious, visible

10. **included**   existing, usual, above, extra

67.   The Gentle Giant

Put the following words in the correct column below:

Word bank: brutal, calm, controlled, savage, pleasant, fierce, cruel, tame, vicious, mild, wild, passive, ferocious, peaceful, harsh, callous, timid, tender

violent	gentle

68.   Synonyms

Choose the synonym` of the word in bold.

1. **white**   colourless, dirty, purity, black

2. **nimble**   alive, agile, fast, amenable

3. **haughty**   humble, attention, arrogant, stern

4. **sanction**   penalty, agree, reject, valid

5. **borderline**   outside, succeed, marginal, merge

6. **correct**   rectify, cure, perpetuate, assess

7. **bargain**   reduced, negotiate, argue, feud

8. **attack**   complain, reason, anger, assault

9. **startled**   imitate, alarmed, terrified, reassure

10. **cabinet**   ministers, bench, board, cupboard

69.   Antonyms

Complete the antonym of the word in bold.

1. **young**   e l _ _ _ _ y

2. **invade**   d e _ _ _ _

3. **select**   r e _ _ _ t

4. **bold**   t i _ _ _

5. **sunset**   s u n _ _ _ _

6. **summer**   w i _ _ _ r

7. **build**   d e m _ _ _ _ h

8. **lie**   s t _ _ _

9. **top**   b _ _ e

10. **reactive**   i n _ _ _

70.   Mind your Ps and Qs

Put the following words in the correct column below:

Word bank: impolite, polite, respectful, decent, insulting, vulgar, cordial, deferential, coarse, considerate, crude, obscene, insolent, gracious

rude	courteous
_____	_____
_____	_____
_____	_____
_____	_____
_____	_____
_____	_____
_____	_____

Which word in the word bank is also
a type of drink?   _____

71.   Synonyms

Complete the synonym of the word in bold.

1. **pointy**   s _ _ r _

2. **fast**   h _ _ t _

3. **late**   d e _ _ _ e d

4. **hurt**   i n _ _ _ e

5. **draw**   s k _ _ _ h

6. **coat**   j a _ _ _ _

7. **cookery**   c u _ _ _ n e

8. **envy**   j e _ _ _ _ s

9. **foam**   f r _ _ _

10. **fret**   w o _ _ _

72.   Antonyms

Choose the antonym of the word in bold.

1. **conform**   comply, coordinate, surrender, oppose

2. **absurd**   sensible, clever, strange, often

3. **potent**   strong, convincing, weak, restless

4. **pretentious**   conceited, modest, reserved, fake

5. **malicious**   kind, nasty, naïve, evade

6. **encrypt**   encode, translate, decode, above

7. **abundance**   plenty, scarcity, never, almost

8. **precarious**   hazardous, harmless, innocuous, secure

9. **constant**   variable, steady, uniform, increases

10. **irrational**   confused, logical, obscure, obvious

73.   A Wobble

Put the following words in the correct column below:

Word bank: hard, rigid, pliable, solid, pliant, soft, vulnerable, stiff, sturdy, weak, wobbly, flexible, tough, inflexible, steadfast, supple

firm	unstable
_____	_____
_____	_____
_____	_____
_____	_____
_____	_____
_____	_____
_____	_____
_____	_____

74. Synonyms

Choose the synonym of the word in bold.

1. **beach**   wave, holiday, cliff, shore

2. **gem**   rock, gold, metal, jewel

3. **prepared**   ready, read, poise, chopped

4. **storm**   windy, torrent, tempest, sand

5. **waver**   hover, hesitate, pseudo, flexible

6. **shivering**   sobbing, trembling, freezing, twinkle

7. **explore**   investigate, look, journey, value

8. **ignite**   blaze, kindle, flicker, move

9. **cook**   create, serve, chef, baked

10. **meek**   meagre, docile, calm, sullen

75.   Antonyms

Complete the antonym of the word in bold.

1. **speak**   l i _ _ _ _

2. **amplify**   r e _ _ _ _

3. **objective**   _ _ _ _ e c t i v e

4. **son**   d a _ _ _ _ e r

5. **hill**   _ _ _ l e y

6. **cherish**   n e _ _ _ _ t

7. **generous**   s e _ _ _ _ h

8. **stagnate**   p r _ _ _ _ s s

9. **obscure**   o b v _ _ _ s

10. **elongate**   c u r _ _ _ l

76. Old and New

Put the following words in the correct column below:

Word bank: modern, antique, ancient, novel, contemporary,
current, mature, veteran, recent, aged

new	old
_____	_____
_____	_____
_____	_____
_____	_____
_____	_____

Which word also means a flow of electricity? _____

77.   Synonyms

Complete the synonym of the word in bold.

1. **funny**   w i _ _ _

2. **reside**   d w _ _ _

3. **jerk**   t w _ _ _ _

4. **contemporary**   _ _ _ e r n

5. **champion**   _ _ _ t o r

6. **severe**   a c _ _ _

7. **inn**   h o s _ _ _

8. **chore**   e _ _ _ _ d

9. **revolve**   o _ _ _ t

10. **peril**   t h _ _ _ _

78.   Antonyms

Choose the antonym of the word in bold.

1. **pious**   holy, godly, sincere, irreverent

2. **wholesome**   partial, entire, uncut, unhealthy

3. **swift**   bird, fly, slow, walk

4. **mellow**   rich, shallow, deep, harsh

5. **mock**   fake, genuine, ridicule, faux

6. **live**   breathe, survive, recording, exist

7. **platonic**   friendly, romantic, pal, mate

8. **detrimental** beneficial, worsen, damage, harm

9. **queasy**   nauseous, well, uneasy, happy

10. **practical**   unfeasible, prudent, athletic, learn

79.   A Simple Conundrum

Put the following words in the correct column below:

Word bank: straight forward, complicated, difficult, perplexing, plain, uncomplicated, easy, convoluted, elaborate, facile, basic, involved, cinch, challenging, intricate

simple	complex

Which word can mean folded, twisted or coiled? _____

80.   Synonyms

Choose the synonym of the word in bold.

1. **serene**   tranquil, cheerful, positive, hopeful

2. **paltry**   memoir, meagre, birds, feathers

3. **bedlam**   sleep, restless, chaos, disprove

4. **favoured**   privileged, unpopular, choice, prejudice

5. **oscillate**   fixed, fluctuate, unmoving, spiral

6. **impediment** assistance, structure, obstacle, safety

7. **imperative** inessential, pressing, desired, critical

8. **assert**   decide, deny, claim, choose

9. **acrid**   pungent, smell, advocate, bitter

10. **toiled**   relaxed, idled, stopped, slaved

81.   Antonyms

Complete the antonym of the word in bold.

1. **absolve**   c o n _ _ _ _

2. **undo**   _ _ _ t e n

3. **deceit**   h o n _ _ _ _ _

4. **specific**   v a _ _ _

5. **obsolete**   c u _ _ _ _ t

6. **fight**   t r u _ _

7. **competent**   i n e _ _

8. **including**   _ _ _ e p t

9. **child**   _ _ _ l t

10. **help**   h i _ _ _ _

82. To Put Asunder

Put the following words in the correct column below:

> Word bank: include, merge, disconnect, divide, sever, join, dissociate, encompass, blend, fuse, isolate, incorporate, scatter, partition, detach, unite

combine	separate
_____	_____
_____	_____
_____	_____
_____	_____
_____	_____
_____	_____
_____	_____
_____	_____

83.   Synonyms

Complete the synonym of the word in bold.

1. **drip**   t r _ _ k _ _

2. **restrict**   c o n _ _ _ _ _

3. **whole**   e n t _ _ _

4. **charm**   t r i _ _ _ t

5. **affable**   f r i _ _ _ _ y

6. **commodity**   p _ _ d _ _ t

7. **cure**   h _ _ _

8. **assemble**   c o m p _ _ _

9. **biography**   m e m _ _ _

10. **mirage**   i l _ _ _ _ o n

88.   Large and Small

Put the following words in the correct column below:

Word bank: big, huge, little, slight, tiny, substantial, immense, enormous, colossal, miniature, massive, microscopic, nanoscopic, miniscule, mammoth, vast, wee, tiddly, teeny, gigantic, stupendous, paltry, mountainous, petite, gargantuan, trifling

large	small
_____	_____
_____	_____
_____	_____
_____	_____
_____	_____
_____	_____
_____	_____
_____	_____
_____	_____
_____	_____
_____	_____
_____	_____

89.   Synonyms

Complete the synonym of the word in bold.

1. **royal**   m a _ _ _ _ i c

2. **kingdom**   e m _ _ _ e

3. **series**   s e _ _ _ _ _ e

4. **maintain**   s _ _ _ a i n

5. **foreign**   a l _ _ _

6. **avoid**   e v _ _ _

7. **desire**   a s p _ _ _

8. **gullible**   n a _ _ _

9. **artefact**   o b _ _ _ t

10. **shorten**   _ _ _ _ e v i a t e

90.   Antonyms

Choose the antonym of the word in bold.

1. **deny**   cautious, affirm, solid, help

2. **tenuous**   hand, provide, strong, slim

3. **jaded**   green, blue, ornamental, enthusiastic

4. **tempt**   appear, discourage, guise, lure

5. **uniform**   clothes, leisure, contrast, even

6. **void**   empty, full, valid, charm

7. **frivolous**   trivial, idle, calm, serious

8. **sagacious**   herb, herbal, wise, foolish

9. **snub**   censure, include, neglect, shame

10. **cheerful**   glum, glad, smirk, mellow

91.   A Little Give and Take

Put the following words in the correct column below:

Word bank: get, furnish, grant, capture, seize, present, yield,
supply, award, catch, apprehend, remove, provide, steal, deliver, pilfer,
contribute, purloin, occupy, impart

give	take
_____	_____
_____	_____
_____	_____
_____	_____
_____	_____
_____	_____
_____	_____
_____	_____
_____	_____

92. Synonyms

Choose the synonym of the word in bold.

1. **versus**   poem, stanza, refrain, against

2. **resonate**   agree, echo, again, shatter

3. **diplomatic**   politics, ambassador, tactful, mild

4. **rock**   sway, move, magma, hard

5. **vouch**   stand, stamp, attest, coupon

6. **dais**   speak, podium, period, era

7. **cup**   beaker, tea, jug, urn

8. **thread**   needle, sew, twist, fibre

9. **celestial**   bicycle, heavenly, singing, vital

10. **exchange**   swap, currency, converge, money

93.   Antonyms

Complete the antonym of the word in bold.

1. **impede**   a s _ _ _ t

2. **calm**   p a _ _ _

3. **bright**   g l _ _ _ y

4. **peak**   t r o _ _ _

5. **robust**   f r a _ _ _ _

6. **coil**   u n r _ _ _ _

7. **lying**   s t _ _ _ _ n g

8. **past**   f _ _ _ _ e

9. **vice**   v i _ _ _ e

10. **destroy**   _ r _ _ t _

94.   Lukewarm

Put the following words in the correct column below:

Word bank:
Word bank: hot, cool, freezing, chilled, boiling, blazing, scorching, icy, sweltering, frosty, scalding, frigid, arctic, tepid

warm	cold
_____	_____
_____	_____
_____	_____
_____	_____
_____	_____
_____	_____
_____	_____

Which word would be the best synonym of lukewarm? _____

95.　Synonyms

Complete the synonym of the word in bold.

1. **idea**　　　n o _ _ _ n

2. **scowl**　　f r _ _ _

3. **hamper**　 b a s _ _ _

4. **stroll**　　 r a m _ _ _

5. **husk**　　　s h _ _ _

6. **fragile**　　b r _ _ _ l e

7. **incline**　　s l _ _ _

8. **physician**　d o _ _ _ _ _

9. **clap**　　　 a p _ _ _ _ d

10. **jam**　　　 c o n _ _ _ _ e

96.   Antonyms

Choose the antonym of the word in bold.

1. **hind**   peel, back, prior, front

2. **robust**   healthy, strong, feeble, hardy

3. **acquire**   obtain, receive, forfeit, procure

4. **midst**   outside, among, middle, thick

5. **drip**   torrent, drop, hail, arid

6. **systematic** methodical, particular, odd, random

7. **sold**   brought, bought, bargain, deplete

8. **cowardice**   alarm, strength, divulge, valour

9. **bury**   funeral, live, unearth, spade

10. **sedate**   waken, woke, choose, elect

97.   A Trifling Matter

Put the following words in the correct column below:

Word bank: significant, inconsequential, minor, vital, superficial, principal, requisite, negligible, substantial, paltry, trifling, required, necessary, fundamental, petty, trivial, indispensable, essential, insignificant, unimportant, critical, immaterial, salient, frivolous

important	irrelevant
_____	_____
_____	_____
_____	_____
_____	_____
_____	_____
_____	_____
_____	_____
_____	_____
_____	_____
_____	_____
_____	_____

98. Synonyms

Choose the synonym of the word in bold.

1. **difficulty**   ordeal, hard, easy, complex

2. **solace**   sun, space, comfort, discord

3. **account**   money, chronicle, diary, bank

4. **prompt**   speech, seed, immediate, identify

5. **sponsor**   charity, employer, donate, fund

6. **essay**   difficult, article, paltry, problem

7. **bland**   spicy, dazzle, insipid, enchant

8. **rot**   decay, stale, fresh, musty

9. **whine**   drink, alcohol, grape, moan

10. **surmise**   deduct, proof, certainty, theory

99.   Synonyms

Complete the synonym of the word in bold.

1. **increase**   b o _ _ t

2. **demand**   i n s _ _ _

3. **adapt**   a _ j _ _ t

4. **comprehensive**   t h _ _ _ _ g h

5. **skim**   b r _ _ _ e

6. **pare**   t r _ _

7. **quick**   s u _ d _ _

8. **punish**   r e b _ _ _

9. **bear**   e n d _ _ _

10. **device**   g a _ _ _ t

100.   Cut-Price Deals

Put the following words in the correct column below:

Word bank: costly, cheap, exorbitant, inexpensive, modest, lavish, profligate, budget, bargain, overpriced, indulgent, thrifty, prudent, expensive

extravagant	economical
_____	_____
_____	_____
_____	_____
_____	_____
_____	_____
_____	_____
_____	_____

Which word is a synonym for wise? _____

Answers

1. Laugh or Cry

Laugh – giggle, chortle, chuckle, guffaw, snicker, crack up, cackle

Cry – weep, sob, wail, bawl, howl, snivel, mewl

2. Synonyms

1. tardy, 2. broad, 3. peak, 4. agree, 5. ajar, 6. tolerant, 7. mix, 8. shabby, 9. caption, 10. insolent

3. Antonyms

1. correct, 2. ignore, 3. worst, 4. conclude, 5. deny, 6. merge, 7. vertical, 8. filthy, 9. repair, 10. object

4. Happy and Sad

Happy – content, joyful, cheerful, glad, pleased, upbeat, elated, jubilant, delighted, gleeful

Sad – upset, miserable, pitiful, lament, distress, depressed, melancholy, dismayed, desolate, glum

Also means – content, lament

5. Synonyms

1. messy, 2. award, 3. interval, 4. level, 5. intelligent, 6. enthusiastic, 7. swallow, 8. consider, 9. tint, 10. desire

6. Antonyms

1. soft, 2. freeze, 3. innocent, 4. perpendicular, 5. final, 6. reward,
7. wavy, 8. gentle, 9. dull, 10. slack

7. Lots and Few

Lots – numerous, plentiful, plenty, myriad, many, populous, several, oodles, copious

Few – lean, slight, trifle, scanty, meagre, negligible, paltry, sparse, scarce

8. Synonyms

1. take, 2. surround, 3. improve, 4. lady, 5. assured, 6. channel,
7. warp, 8. soiled, 9.misplace, 10. discuss

9. Antonyms

1. subtle, 2. opaque, 3. shrink, 4. profit, 5. float, 6. unique,
7. drowsy, 8. modest, 9. sweet, 10. cease

10. Wise Folly

Smart – clever, bright, intelligent, wise, shrews, astute, brilliant, genius, savvy, sage

Stupid – dumb, doltish, dopey, silly, witless, imbecile, unintelligent, inane, unwise, ludicrous

11. Synonyms

1. dozen, 2, raise, 3 dread, 4. fable, 5. discover, 6. tranquil,
7. evaluation, 8. deceive, 9. option, 10. certain

12. Antonyms

1. illusion, 2. betray, 3. nervous, 4. gullible, 5. complex, 6. brittle, 7. shuffle, 8. partial, 9. conceal, 10. sparse

13. Movement

Move – mobile, motion, active, ambulatory, locomotive

Still – stationary, inaction, immobile, stable, stagnant

Also means – mobile, stagnant, stable

Homophone – stationery

14. Synonyms

1. hook, 2. anguish, 3. subsequent, 4. cruel, 5. achievable, 6. comprehend, 7. twine, 8. reveal, 9. marginal, 10. blend

15. Antonyms

1. mature, 2. caught, 3. doubt, 4. follow, 5. accept, 6. chaos, 7. guilty, 8. sweet, 9. empty, 10. tangle

16. Hungry and Sated

Hungry – ravenous, peckish, starving, famished

Sated – full, replete, satisfied, satiated

Which word – peckish, satisfied, replete, satiated

17. Synonyms

1. drowsy, 2. abandon, 3. battle, 4. concise, 5. persuade, 5. giant,
7. frugal, 8. chemist, 9. victory, 10. exhaust

18. Antonyms

1. elevate, 2. agree, 3. dynamic, 4. dead, 5. inept, 6. mediocre,
7. irrational, 8. compulsory, 9. dextrous, 10. lenient

19. Approximately Spot-on

Exact – precise, accurate, perfect, specific, detailed, definite, meticulous, rigorous, sharp, scrupulous

Vague – obscure, undefined, faint, shadowy, ambiguous, dubious, equivocal, uncertain, unclear, nebulous

20. Synonyms

1. restrain, 2. chastise, 3. deplete, 4. resist, 5. surplus, 6. penetrate,
7. establish, 8. copy, 9. flexible, 10. confuse

21. Antonyms

1. release, 2. retreat, 3. insult, 4. amateur, 5. attic, 6. comedy,
7. opaque, 8. defeat, 9. private, 10. depart

22. When?

Before – former, prior, earlier, ahead, previously, preliminary

After – subsequently, later, afterwards, ensuing, succeeding, thereafter

He prepared thoroughly ahead of time.

23. Synonyms

1. remove, 2. easy, 3. crash, 4. shack, 5. possess, 6. infant,
7. present, 8. tardy, 9. sudden, 10. fair

24. Antonyms

1. sustain, 2. odd, 3. soothe, 4. confirm, 5. agitated, 6. expert, 7. upset,
8. deter, 9. major, 10. wisdom

25. Let's Clean Up

Clean – clear, unclouded, uncontaminated, neat, pristine, washed

Dirt – filth, soil, contaminate, dingy, grime, stain

Which word – soil, pristine

26. Synonyms

1. loud, 2. lazy 3. dingy, 4. avoid, 5. abstain, 6. baton, 7. decline,
8. stormy, 9. deserted, 10. ask

27. Antonyms

1. tight, 2. timid, 3. natural, 4. frown, 5. urban, 6. defend, 7. ceiling,
8. export, 9. cloudy, 10. borrow

28. Break a Leg

Lucky – fortunate, favourable, felicitous, prosperous, fortuitous, blessed

Unlucky – unfortunate, unfavourable, doomed, ill-fated, luckless, hapless,

Break a leg means good luck.

29. Synonyms

1. middle, 2. loyal, 3. feeble, 4. volume, 5. abroad, 6. transform, 7. gather, 8. sprint, 9. sparkle, 10. mimic

30. Antonyms

1. biased, 2. deprive, 3. dawn, 4. humid, 5. plant, 6. failure, 7. opponent, 8. sink, 9. praise, 10. inferior

31. No Sitting on the Fence

Agree – concur, accord, tally, concord, match, consent, accept, assent

Disagree – differ, dissent, discord, refuse, contradict, diverge, clash, counter

To sit on the fence means to not take sides.

32. Synonyms

1. disagreeable, 2. eager, 3. operate, 4. allowance, 5. order, 6. argue, 7. far, 8. position, 9. component, 10. perfect

33. Antonyms

1. noon, 2. spend, 3. junior, 4. consonant, 5. funny, 6. blunt, 7. seldom, 8. woman, 9. sombre, 10. toasty

34. By and By, in the Fullness of Time

Now – immediately, today, instantly, straightaway, directly, forthwith

Sometime – whenever, someday, intermittently, occasional, periodically, sporadically

Which word - periodically

35. Synonyms

1. despise, 2. relative, 3. predict, 4. consider, 5. solitude, 6. exile, 7. crowd, 8. talent, 9. distant, 10. gather

36. Antonyms

1. reckless, 2. safe, 3. secret, 4. dishonest, 5. liberal, 6. include, 7. futile, 8. like, 9. dim, 10. smother

37. I'm Rather Partial to Fractions

Fraction – part, piece, section, sector, division, fragment

Whole – complete, entire, total, altogether, unit, full

Homophone - piece

38. Synonyms

1. pleasant, 2. thoughtful, 3. distant, 4. force, 5. slander, 6. fair, 7. elite, 8. attack, 9. float, 10. mist

39. Antonyms

1. better, 2. guest, 3. withdraw, 4. acute, 5. cheerful, 6. extend, 7. pause, 8. labour, 9. concise, 10. discard

40. Ready for bed

Tired – weary, fatigue, jaded, exhausted, drained, drowsy

Energised – lively, fresh, activated, invigorated, refreshed, rested

Which word – exhausted, fresh

41. Synonyms

1. donate, 2. choose, 3. loose, 4. error. 5. heap, 6. unusual, 7. floppy, 8. might, 9. vital, 10. swift

42. Antonyms

1. copious, 2. obscure, 3. crave, 4. refused, 5. land, 6. care, 7. permit, 8. flimsy, 9. rush, 10. Refute68

43. At the Marketplace

Buy – purchase, acquire, get, invest, obtain, procure

Sell – market, auction, peddle, hawk, stock, vend

Which word – hawk

44. Synonyms

1. deform, 2. important, 3. recognise, 4. tireless, 5. humble, 6. barrier, 7. earnest, 8. pleasant, 9. annoying, 10. proof

45. Antonyms

1. ancestor, 2. ignorance 3. adjacent, 4. awkward, 5. interrupt, 6. dense, 7. forget, 8. oblivious, 9. oppose, 10. poverty

46. Bigger and Smaller

Expand – grow, inflate, amplify, enlarge, dilate, magnify

Contract – shrink, deflate, compress, constrict, compact, reduce

Which word – amplify, inflate

47. Synonyms

1. cleanse, 2. bizarre, 3. obstruct, 4. reveal, 5. manual, 6. meadow,
7. pinnacle, 8. modify, 9. endure, 10. replace

48. Antonyms

1. interior, 2. discreet, 3. obey, 4. oppress, 5. foreign, 6. solace, 7. capture,
8. inflame, 9. blunt, 10. enable

49. Good, Better, Best

Good – nice, pleasant, delightful, gratifying, marvellous, sterling, proficient,
adept, beneficial, agreeable

Bad – nasty, vile, horrible, despicable, foul, obnoxious, repulsive,
loathsome, odious, atrocious

50. Synonyms

1. basis, 2. hesitant, 3. crack, 4. riveting, 5. camouflage, 6. dramatic, 7. add,
8. adolescent, 9. yearn, 10. obvious

51. Antonyms

1. vacant, 2. seldom, 3. demand, 4. debit, 5. promote, 6. poetry, 7. tense,
8. hollow, 9. shallow, 10 entrance

52. Bone Idle

Active – industrious, conscientious, diligent, productive, busy, tireless. assiduous

Lazy – inactive, slack, idle, indolent, lackadaisical, unproductive, lax

53. Synonyms

1. visible, 2. dwindle, 3. devout, 4. accuse, 5. endure, 6. height, 7. furious, 8. verify, 9. construct, 10. certain

54. Antonyms

1. tidy, 2. illegal, 3. superior, 4. ordered, 5. irritate, 6. wild, 7. impossible, 8. conventional, 9. wane, 10. frugal

55. In Need of Repair

Damage – break, fracture, rupture, harm, impair, wreck

Repair – fix, mend, patch, reconstruct, improve, restore

Also means – break, fix

56. Synonyms

1. limit, 2. transport, 3. unusual, 4. budget, 5. balance, 6. clearly, 7. rough, 8. dazzling, 9. splendid, 10. compliment

57. Antonyms

1. intentional, 2. lowly, 3. customer, 4. voluntary, 5. mature, 6. descend, 7. conclude, 8. right, 9. tenant, 10. increase

58. Open and Shut

Opening – aperture, cavity, cleft, crack, crevice, cut, fissure, hatch, rift, rupture, slit, slot, tear, vent

Closed – sealed, shut, impenetrable, impermeable, blocked, firm, tight, secure, impervious, fixed, fast, fastened, corked, locked

59. Synonyms

1. include, 2. concur, 3. remedy, 4. hopeful, 5. ramble, 6. regal, 7. petty, 8. submerge, 9. decode, 10. attic

60 Antonyms

1. validate, 2. sanction, 3. interest, 4. minimal, 5. tedious, 6. discontinue, 7. able, 8. loyalty, 9. good, 10. despise

61. There's no doubt

Confidence – assurance, certainty, boldness, fortitude, fearlessness, grit

Doubt – fear, hesitation, uncertainty, cowardice, timidity, apprehension

Which word – grit

62. Synonyms

1. receive, 2. confidential, 3. maze, 4. essential, 5. additional, 6. thick, 7. bloated, 8. harbour, 9. inherited, 10. obvious

63. Antonyms

1. wrong, 2. dissuade, 3. conclusion, 4. pleased, 5. punctual, 6. neglect, 7. present, 8. variable, 9. thrive, 10. sturdy

64. To love

Love – adore, cherish, fondness, besotted, relish, admire

Hate – despise, animosity, dislike, enmity, abhor, loathe

Which word – relish

65. Synonyms

1. certain, 2. company, 3. gigantic, 4. pupil, 5. instruct, 6. alright, 7. scene,
8. ticket, 9. foolish, 10. leapt

66. Antonyms

1. uplift, 2. agreeable, 3. always, 4. stale, 5. accept, 6. supple, 7. lowly,
8. wrinkled, 9. vague, 10. extra

67. The Gentle Giant

Violent – brutal, savage, fierce, cruel, vicious, wild, ferocious, harsh, callous

Gentle – calm, controlled, pleasant, tame, mild, passive, peaceful, timid,
tender

68. Synonyms

1. colourless, 2. agile, 3. arrogant, 4. penalty, 5. marginal, 6. rectify,
7. negotiate, 8. assault, 9. alarmed, 10. cupboard

69. Antonyms

1. elderly, 2. defend, 3. reject, 4. timid, 5. sunrise, 6. winter, 7. demolish,
8. stand, 9. base, 10. inert

70. Mind your Ps and Qs

Rude – impolite, insulting, vulgar, coarse, crude, obscene, insolent

Courteous – polite, respectful, decent, cordial, deferential, considerate, gracious

Which word – cordial

71. Synonyms

1. sharp, 2. hasty, 3. delayed, 4. injure, 5. sketch, 6. jacket, 7. cuisine, 8. jealous, 9. froth, 10. worry

72. Antonyms

1. oppose, 2. sensible, 3. weak, 4. modest, 5. kind, 6. decode, 7. scarcity, 8. secure, 9. variable, 10. logical

73. A Wobble

Firm – hard, rigid, solid, stiff, sturdy, tough, inflexible, steadfast

Unstable – pliable, pliant, soft, vulnerable, weak, wobbly, flexible, supple

74. Synonyms

1. shore, 2. jewel, 3. ready, 4. tempest, 5. hesitate, 6. trembling, 7. investigate, 8. kindle, 9. chef, 10. docile

75. Antonyms

1. listen, 2. reduce, 3. subjective, 4. daughter, 5. valley, 6. neglect, 7. selfish, 8. progress, 9. obvious, 10. curtail

76. Old and New

New – modern, novel, contemporary, current, recent

Old – antique, ancient, mature, veteran, aged

Which word – current

77. Synonyms

1. witty, 2. dwell, 3. twitch, 4. modern, 5. victor, 6. acute, 7. hostel, 8. errand, 9. orbit, 10. threat

78. Antonyms

1. irreverent, 2. unhealthy, 3. slow, 4. harsh, 5. genuine, 6. recording, 7. romantic, 8. beneficial, 8. well, 10. unfeasible

79. A Simple Conundrum

Simple – straight forward, plain, uncomplicated, easy, facile, basic, cinch

Complex – complicated, difficult, perplexing, convoluted, elaborate, involved, challenging, intricate

Which word – convoluted

80. Synonyms

1. tranquil, 2. meagre, 3. chaos, 4. privileged, 5. fluctuate, 6. obstacle, 7. critical, 8. claim, 9. pungent, 10. slaved

81. Antonyms

1. condemn, 2. fasten, 3. honesty, 4. vague, 5. current, 6. truce, 7. inept, 8. except, 9. adult, 10. hinder

82. To Put Asunder

Combine – include, merge, join, encompass, blend, fuse, incorporate, unite

Separate – disconnect, divide, sever, dissociate, isolate, scatter, partition, detach

83. Synonyms

1. trickle, 2. confine, 3. entire, 4. trinket, 5. friendly, 6. product, 7. heal, 8. compile, 9. memoir, 10. illusion

84. Antonyms

1. regression, 2. energetic, 3. extravagance, 4. immune, 5. endure, 6. compliant, 7. surplus, 8. fission, 9. elongate, 10. delight

85. Don't get too Cocky

Humble – modest, shy, timid, meek, unpretentious, unassuming, demure

Arrogant – proud, imperious, pompous, pretentious, smug, vain, boastful

Which word – vain

86. Synonyms

1. sweeten, 2. insignia, 3. determined, 4. basic, 5. capability, 6. abstain, 7. countless, 8. winning, 9. fragrant, 10. bother

87. Antonyms

1. cheap. 2. mystery, 3. comfort, 4. adverse, 5. burden, 6. loyalty, 7. decline, 8. efficient, 9. conserve, 10. solitary

88. Large and Small

Large – big, huge, substantial, immense, enormous, colossal, massive, mammoth, vast, gigantic, stupendous, mountainous, gargantuan

Small – little, slight, tiny, miniature, microscopic, nanoscopic, miniscule, wee, tiddly, teeny, paltry, petite, trifling

89. Synonyms

1. majestic, 2. empire, 3. sequence, 4. sustain, 5. alien, 6. evade, 7. aspire, 8. naïve / naive, 9. object, 10. abbreviate

90. Antonyms

1. affirm, 2. strong, 3. enthusiastic, 4. discourage, 5. contrast, 6. full, 7. serious, 8. foolish, 9. include, 10. glum

91. A Little Give and Take

Give – furnish, grant, present, yield, supply, award, provide, deliver, contribute, impart

Take – get, capture, seize, catch, apprehend, remove, steal, pilfer, purloin, occupy

92. Synonyms

1. against, 2. echo, 3. tactful, 4. sway, 5. attest, 6. podium, 7. beaker, 8. fibre, 9. heavenly, 10. swap

93. Antonyms

1. assist, 2. panic, 3. gloomy, 4. trough, 5. fragile, 6. unravel, 7. standing, 8. future, 9. virtue, 10. create

94. Lukewarm

Warm – hot, boiling, blazing, scorching, sweltering, scalding, tepid

Cold – cool, freezing, chilled, icy, frosty, frigid, arctic

Which word – tepid

95. Synonyms

1. notion, 2. frown, 3. basket, 4. ramble, 5. shell, 6. brittle, 7. slope,
8. doctor, 9. applaud, 10. conserve

96. Antonyms

1. front, 2. feeble, 3. forfeit, 4. outside, 5. torrent, 6. random, 7. bought,
8. valour, 9. unearth, 10. waken

97. A Trifling Matter

Important – significant, vital, principal, requisite, substantial, required,
necessary, fundamental, indispensable, essential, critical, salient

Irrelevant – inconsequential, minor, superficial, negligible, paltry, trifling,
petty, trivial, insignificant, unimportant, immaterial, frivolous

98. Synonyms

1. ordeal, 2. comfort, 3. chronicle, 4. immediate, 5. fund, 6. article,
7. insipid, 8. decay, 9. moan, 10. deduct

99. Synonyms

1. boost, 2. insist, 3. adjust, 4. thorough, 5. browse, 6. trim, 7. sudden,
8. rebuke, 9. endure, 10. gadget

100. Cut-Price Deals

Extravagant – costly, exorbitant, lavish, profligate, overpriced, indulgent, expensive

Economical – cheap, inexpensive, modest, budget, bargain, thrifty, prudent

Which word – prudent

Printed in Great Britain
by Amazon